MEL BAY PRESENTS

BARITONE UKULELE SCALES

BY LEE "DREW" ANDREWS

Cover instrument: Kala KA-B Baritone Ukulele.
www.kalaukulele.com

1 2 3 4 5 6 7 8 9 0

© 2009 BY MEL BAY PUBLICATIONS, INC., PACIFIC, MO 63069.
ALL RIGHTS RESERVED. INTERNATIONAL COPYRIGHT SECURED. B.M.I. MADE AND PRINTED IN U.S.A.
No part of this publication may be reproduced in whole or in part, or stored in a retrieval system, or transmitted in any form
or by any means, electronic, mechanical, photocopy, recording, or otherwise, without written permission of the publisher.
Visit us on the Web at www.melbay.com — E-mail us at email@melbay.com

This book is intended for Baritone and Tenor ukuleles in G tuning.

No fingerings were included with these scales. This decision is left up to the player. The multiple fingerings of each scale are shown to better facilitate playing over the entire fretboard.

G tuning = DGBE

Index

Scales and Modes

Special thanks to Mike Upton and Rick Carlson at Kala Ukuleles.

Major / Ionian Scale

Construction: whole step, whole step, half step, whole step, whole step, whole step, half step.

Use: with major chords and chords from the major family (major, 6th, maj. 7, maj. 9, add 9, 6/9).
Also, a major scale can be used with any chord in the major key. For example – use the C major scale with any of the chords in the key of C (C, Dm, Em, F, G, Am, and Bdim).

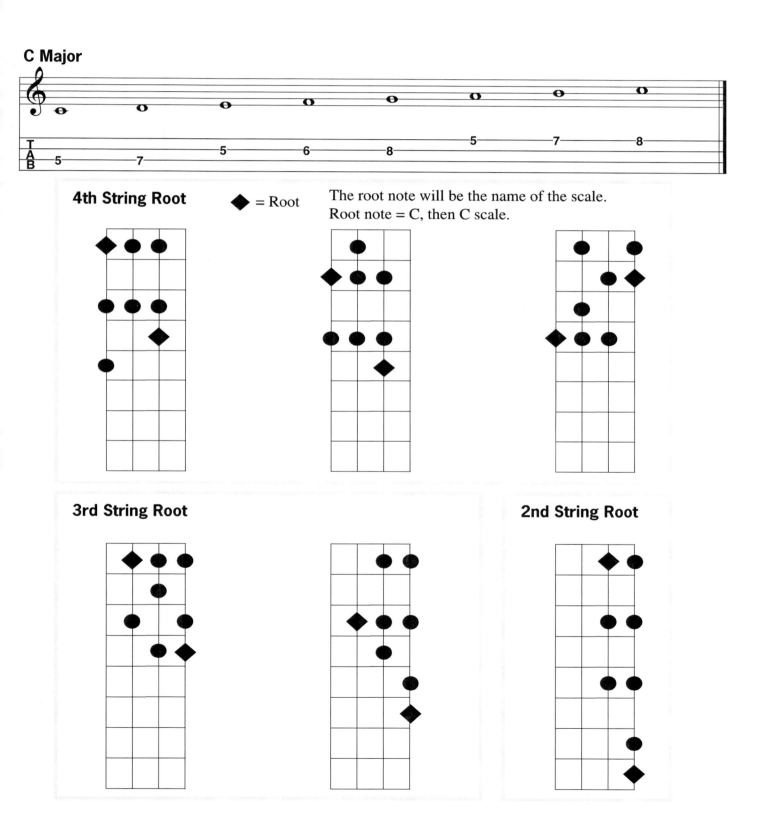

Natural Minor / Aeolian Scale

Construction: major scale with a lowered 3rd, 6th, and 7th.

Use: with minor, m7, or m9 chords.

C Natural Minor

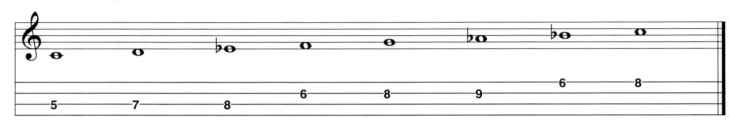

4th String Root   ◆ = Root

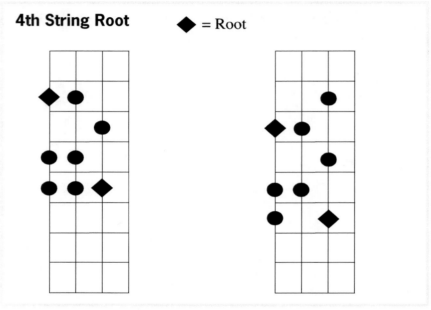

3rd String Root

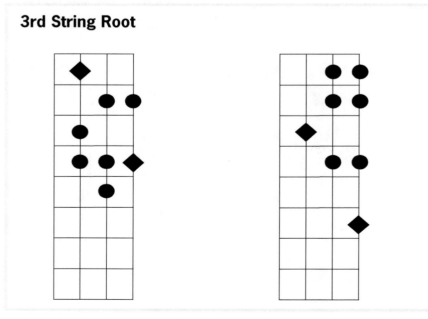

2nd String Root

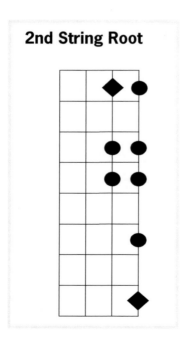

Harmonic Minor Scale

Construction: natural minor scale with a raised 7th.

Use: with minor, m7, m9, m+7, and other chords within a given minor key (A harmonic minor against Am, Bm7♭5, Dm, and E7)

C Harmonic Minor

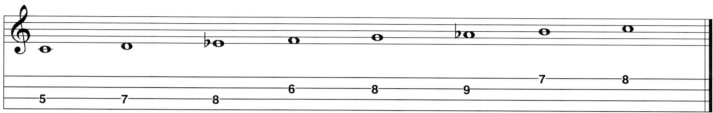

4th String Root

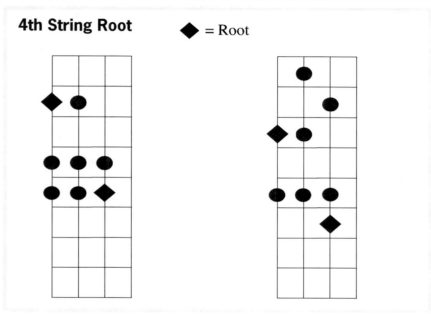

♦ = Root

3rd String Root

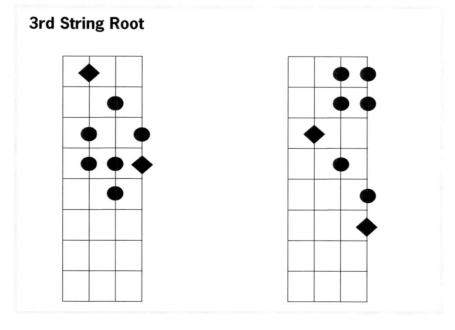

2nd String Root

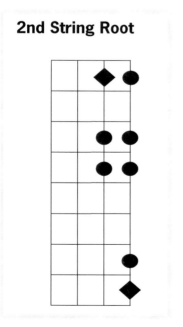

Melodic Minor Scale

Construction: natural minor scale with raised 6th and 7th degrees when ascending and not raised when descending (natural minor when descending).

Use: with minor type chords (minor, m6, m7, m+7, and m9) and other chords within a given minor key.

C Melodic Minor

Major Pentatonic Scale

Construction: major scale with the half steps omitted (omitted 4th and omitted 7th).

Use: with major type chords (major, 6th, maj.7, maj. 9, add 9, and 6/9). Also, the major pentatonic scale can be used against a minor chord whose root is 1½ steps lower than the letter name of the major pentatonic scale.

C Major Pentatonic

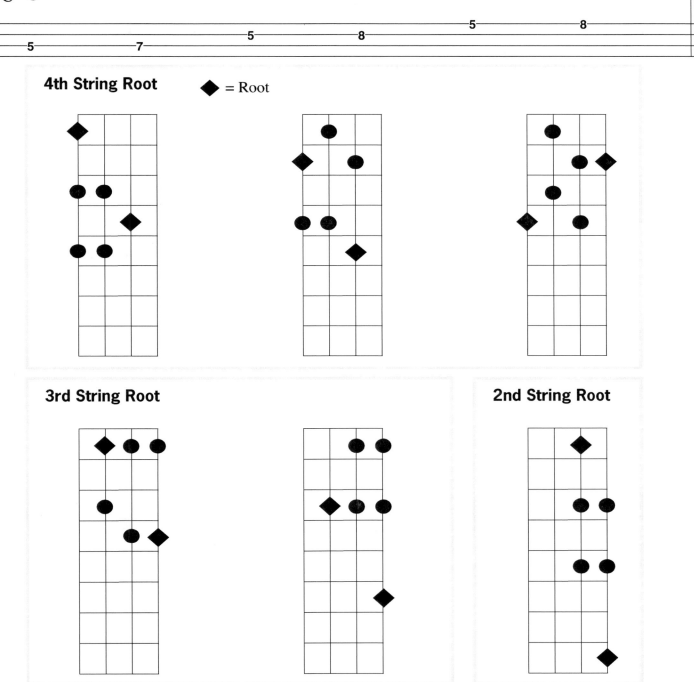

Minor Pentatonic Scale

Construction: natural minor scale with the half steps omitted (omitted 2nd and omitted 6th).

Use: with minor, m7, or m9 chords. Also, the minor pentatonic scale can be played against a major chord whose root is 1½ steps higher than the root of the minor pentatonic scale.

C Minor Pentatonic

4th String Root

◆ = Root

3rd String Root

2nd String Root

The Blues Scale

Construction: root, lowered 3rd, 4th, lowered 5th, natural 5th, and lowered 7th.

Use: with 7th, 9th, 11th, 13th, altered seventh chords (7♭5, 7♯9, etc.), or with any chord in the blues progression. The blues scale which is used should have the same letter name as the key in which the blues is being played. When the chords in the progression change, it is not necessary to change the scale.

C Blues Scale

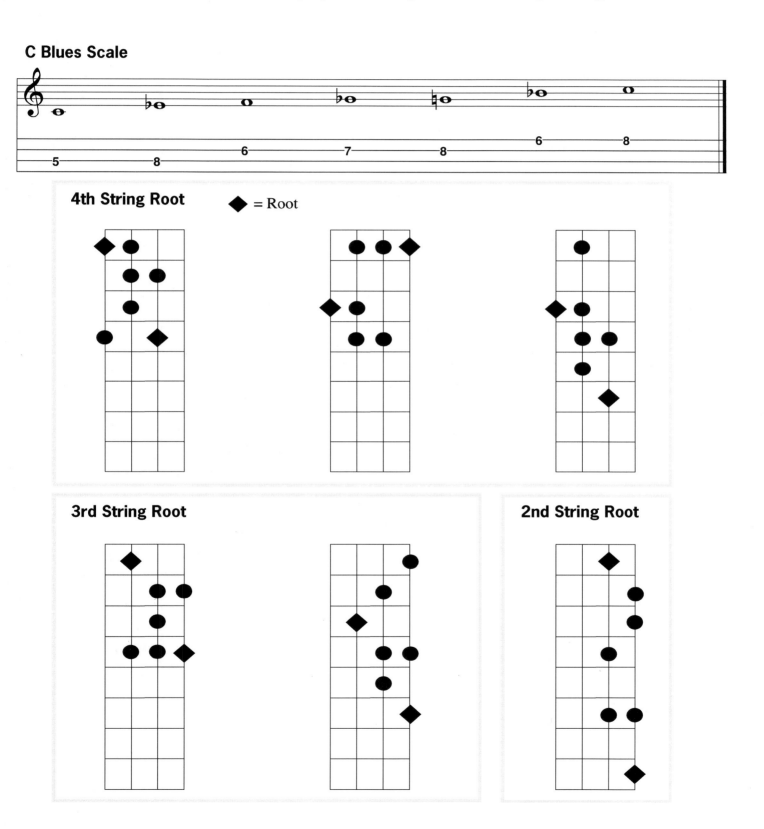

Dorian Mode

Construction: major scale beginning on the second degree (C dorian = B♭ major scale beginning on the C note)

C Dorian

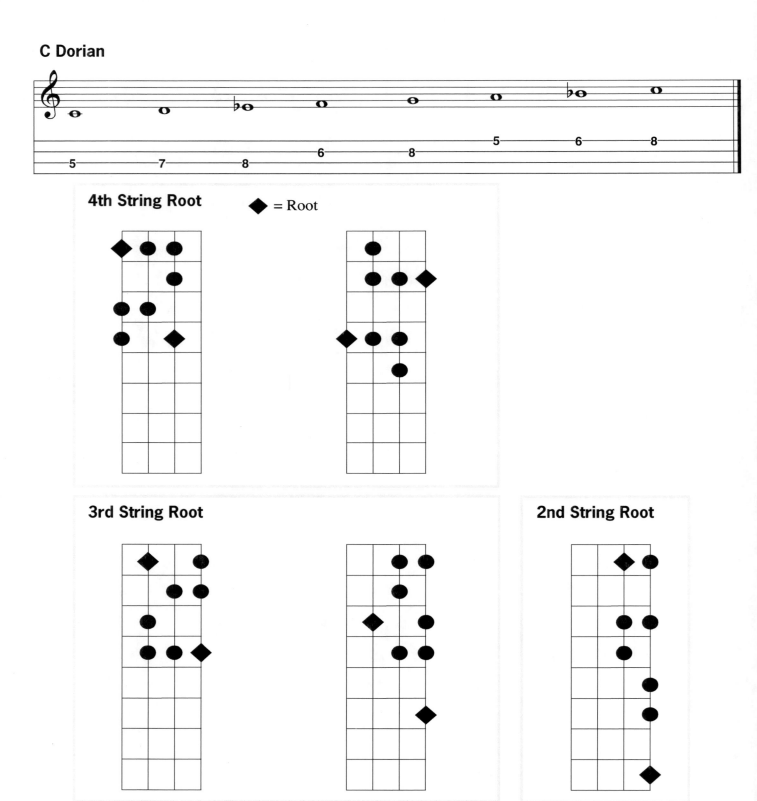

4th String Root   ◆ = Root

3rd String Root

2nd String Root

Mixolydian Mode

Construction: major scale beginning on the fifth degree (major scale with a lowered 7th).

Use: with 7th, 9th, 11th, and 13th chords.

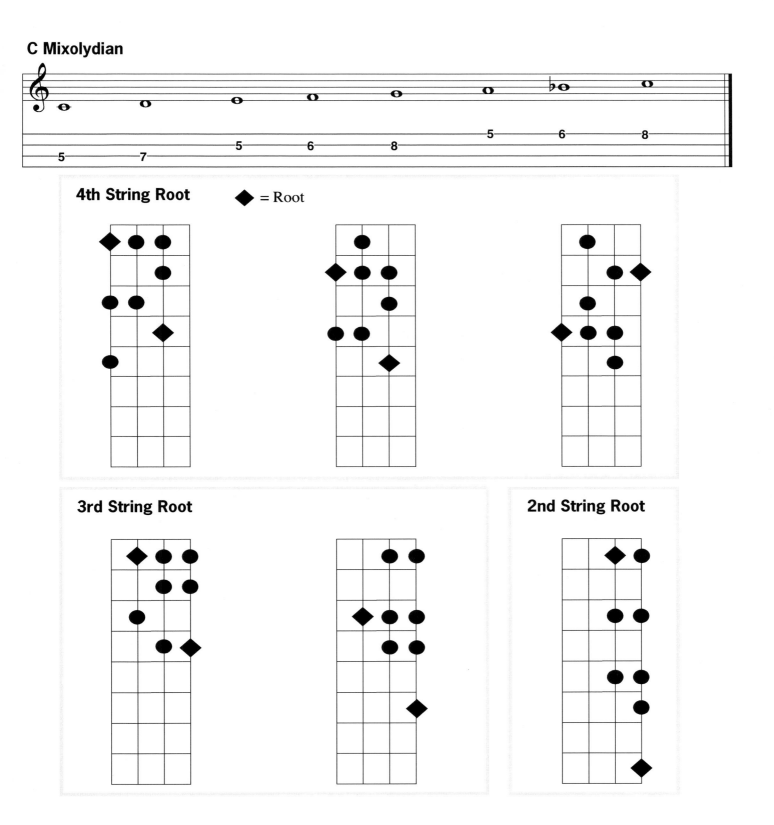

C Mixolydian

4th String Root ◆ = Root

3rd String Root

2nd String Root

Phrygian Mode

Construction: major scale beginning on the third degree (E phrygian = C major scale beginning on the E note).

Use: with minor or m7 chords. To get a Spanish quality, the phrygian mode can also be played against a major chord (i.e., E phrygian against an E chord).

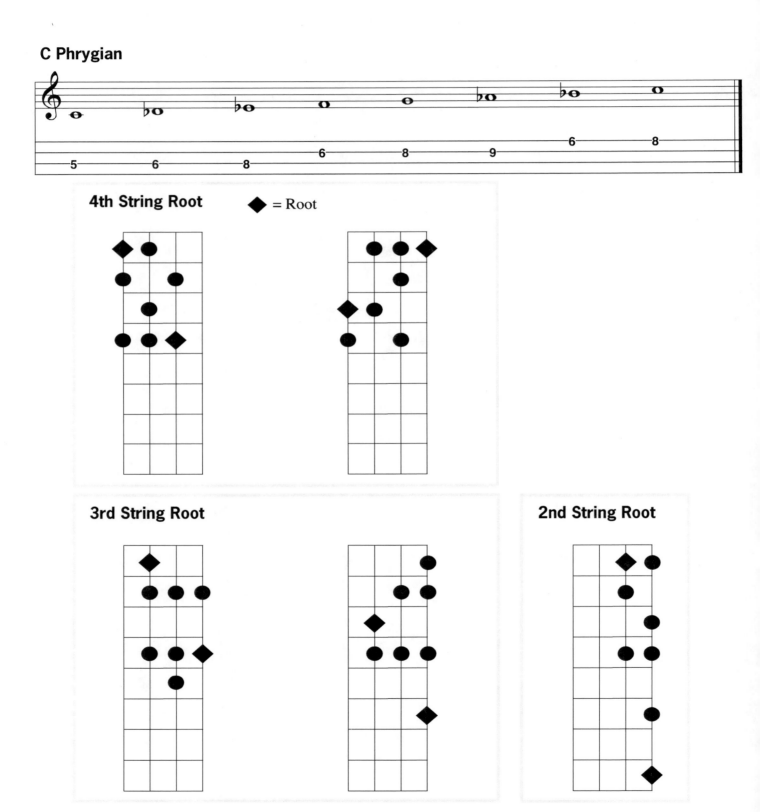

Diminished (Whole-Half)

Construction: whole-step, half-step, whole-step, half-step, etc.

Use: with diminished chords.

C Diminished (Whole-Half)

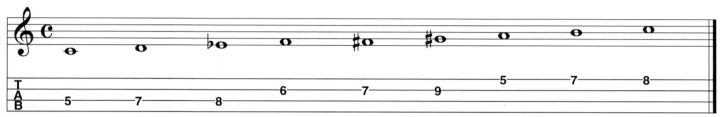

4th String Root   ◆ = Root

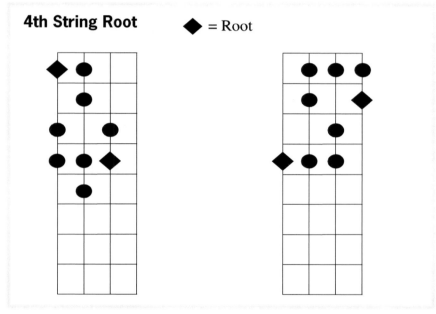

3rd String Root   **2nd String Root**

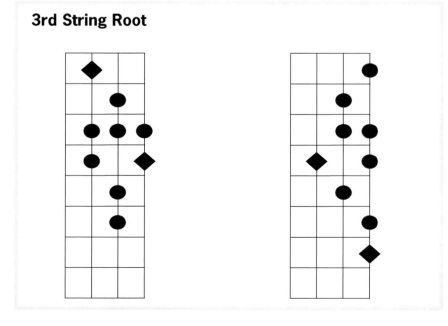
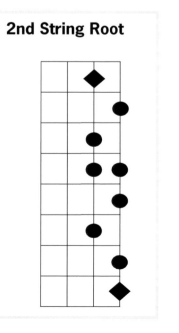

13

Baritone and Tenor Ukeleles
G Tuning

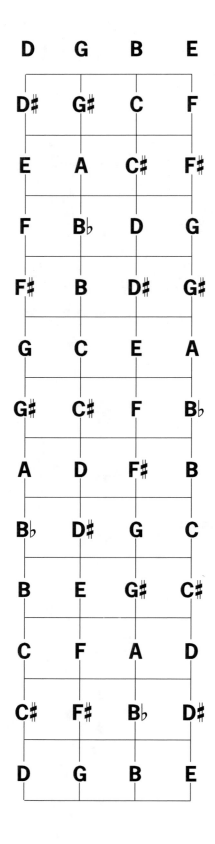

About the Author

Lee "Drew" Andrews is a multi-instrumentalist with a day job. He is head editor at Mel Bay Publications, where he has been for the last 7 years. He has written over twenty best-selling books for ukulele, guitar, mandolin, banjo, Dobro® and more. At the 2009 Winter NAMM show three of his Children's Chord books, one being ukulele, won a Best in Show award.

Drew plays with the Polynesian revue "A Touch of Paradise". He plays ukulele, bass and percussion. With this group he has played for US Senators and Congressmen as well as foreign heads of state. Most recently they played at the International Steel Guitar Convention in St. Louis, Missouri backing up the world-famous Hawaiian steel player L.T. Zinn. Drew is also an in-demand teacher.

Be sure to visit the author's website www.UkuleleVillage.com.

Photo credit: Gary W. Davis